Holy Sparks

Praise for Holy Sparks

"These are poems that are luminous in seeing, and seeking, 'a miracle here, / a miracle there,' refusing at the same time to look away from—or ignore—the shadowed violence that we, as a species, perpetrate toward the creatures who share this earthly home with us. They remind us, with a prophet's fierce eye, that we belong to each other, that we hold our vulnerabilities in common since our fates are inextricably bound together. They also invite us, again and again, to 'keep all day before [us] / the leitmotif of the unflinching / faithful believer bowing to the infinite / Maker and Keeper.' With this new collection, Diane Woodcock establishes herself as one of the voices our culture desperately needs—if we are to treasure the radiant if also fragile beauty that saturates this world, and measure what it might require of us to enter into living dialogue with all this. Only on this path of deep listening and attentive surrendering, she reminds us, will we find the courage to 'elude the deathly solitude, / false images and disembodied / of these times, / instigating hope / by writing the existent— / my final act of resistance.' Despite the often gentle tone of these radiant poems, this is a manifesto calling us to live responsibly, and, while we do, learn to 'pray for a new day when we'll all be worthy / of being created free.' "

—**Mark S. Burrows**, poet and author, *The Wandering Radiance: Selected Poems of Hilde Domin*, and with Jon M. Sweeney, *Meister Eckhart's Book of Darkness and Light: Meditations on the Path of the Wayless Way*

"Nothing escapes exploitation in this world. No matter how much we speak up, it continues. In *Holy Sparks*, Woodcock draws our attention to the destruction. She points out, in the scope of things, why we are here. 'But I am torn, sworn / to do my part though my heart / is broken—all natural entities / suffering.' Isn't it time we take the world back to what it once was? End these atrocities of nature and people? These poems are a powerful reminder of our changing world and what we are facing. Questions are asked, but the answers would require change. It is evident how important this book is."

—**Gloria Mindock**, Editor of Červená Barva Press, award-winning author of *Ash*

"Whatever underlies humanity's unique responsibility for creation—and we might be nuanced about that—the world is replete with wonders to behold and to protect, as we see in Diane Woodcock's markedly detailed eco-encompassing collection *Holy Sparks*. At times cataclysmic, yet valiantly hopeful, the poems are an urgent call to revere our God-given, God-infused yet oft-ravaged world. In language that is both tender and terrifying, Woodcock compels us into contemplation, ever insisting on the value of less over more, stillness over motion, generosity over grasp. In the darkest hour of our over-indulgence, the poet reminds us, to 'make time and space / . . . / for mercy and grace.' And lastly, at the book's closing, we read: 'This is about . . . / doing the noble / liberating thing when / the moment arrives.' For Woodcock, that long-overdue moment for self-emptying veneration has come; it is our cliff-hanging present."

—**Sofia M. Starnes**, author of *The Consequence of Moonlight: Poems*, and other works

"Orbiting our attention from Collared doves to the prophet Mohammad, and from communion wafers to Crab-plovers, Woodcock writes with a fiercely probing grace that affirms the genuine connections between the ecological and the spiritual. While asking often unanswerable questions, this collection shifts between the lightness of being and the 'still point of darkness' with precision and patience. This book is a deeply necessary addition to the ecopoetic landscape."

—**Katy Abrams**, Editor, *Cold Mountain Review*

Holy Sparks

DIANA WOODCOCK

IRON PEN

PARACLETE PRESS
BREWSTER, MASSACHUSETTS

2023 First Printing

Holy Sparks: Poems

Copyright © 2023 by Diane G. Woodcock

ISBN 978-1-64060-601-2

The Iron Pen name and logo are trademarks of Paraclete Press

Library of Congress Cataloging-in-Publication Data

Names: Woodcock, Diana, author.
Title: Holy sparks / by Diana Woodcock.
Other titles: Holy sparks (Compilation)
Description: Brewster, Massachusetts : Paraclete Press, 2023. | Summary: "Holy Sparks is a collection of ecopoetry with a spiritual spin-a call to partake of Earth's wisdom so that we might participate in the Creator's ongoing work"-- Provided by publisher.
Identifiers: LCCN 2023000766 (print) | LCCN 2023000767 (ebook) | ISBN 9781640606012 (trade paperback) | ISBN 9781640606029 (epub) | ISBN 9781640606036 (pdf)
Subjects: BISAC: POETRY / Subjects & Themes / Inspirational & Religious | POETRY / Women Authors | LCGFT: Poetry.
Classification: LCC PS3623.O664 H65 2023 (print) | LCC PS3623.O664 (ebook) | DDC 811/.6--dc23/eng/20230106
LC record available at https://lccn.loc.gov/2023000766
LC ebook record available at https://lccn.loc.gov/2023000767

10 9 8 7 6 5 4 3 2 1

All rights reserved. No portion of this book may be reproduced, stored in an electronic retrieval system, or transmitted in any form or by any means—electronic, mechanical, photocopy, recording, or any other—except for brief quotations in printed reviews, without the prior permission of the publisher.

Published by Paraclete Press
Brewster, Massachusetts
www.paracletepress.com

Printed in the United States of America

Contents

There are holy sparks
in all created beings.

—THOMAS MERTON

Preface

The Ecopoet's Prayer

What are the odds
that any moment now the gods
will grant inspiration?

Still, I prostrate myself
and wait. All I really ask
is to be up to the task

of writing majestically
and puckishly simultaneously
in equal measure, to break down

the false boundary between
human and nonhuman species,
to bend minds, provoke thoughts

about animal sentience and intelligence,
provide evidence humans are not
the center of the universe, arouse

cross-species curiosity, ask
of my reader that s/he invite
the animals, birds and fishes

to teach—inquire,
Aren't you tired of all the false
barriers? All I require

of my reader is this: Drop
the pronoun *it* and adopt s/he;
aspire to a higher level of thinking

about our nonhuman kin; and
consider how our thinking affects
future prospects of each species.

All I ask, my dear reader,
is this: Realize all life is one,
and as the air and oceans go—

and one by one,
each species—so go
us *Homo sapiens*.

I

Called Out by Bulbuls

There are hundreds of ways to kneel and kiss the ground. ~ Rumi

Today I found yet another way
to kneel and pray—set out
a shallow pan filled with water,
a birdbath for the bulbuls.

Got quiet and still,
shut out the unbearable world
to be at home with white-eared softbills,
Pycnonotus leucotis, those precocious

socialites. Together we praised
the silent earth, her dark loam,
mold and sod, dust and dew.
I learned from the bulbuls to do

nothing but sit and sway
on a branch of bougainvillea all day,
just being. *Doing nothing,*
yet nothing left undone.

Abstained from weeding, the heart bleeding
for the most common green shoot.
Quiet and still, just sitting and
considering how the politics of speed

deprive us of our natural habitats.
This little coastal town's turned
upside down, thanks to oil and gas,
air and water pollution.

I sat and meditated, the solution
not so far-fetched—escape the blind
process of proliferation—
participation in third-world

exploitation and pollution.
In solitude and solidarity
with bulbuls, a clarity,
a sense of finitude overwhelms me.

The bulbuls call like chimes
to one another– a sound-map of this
desert town, songline from aridity to sea.
No mountains and moors,

nothing here but low desert terrain,
dunes shifting toward the sea,
a saline body on three sides of me,
and the miswak tree—fruit

upon which bulbuls love to gorge.
The urgency of Carson's silent spring
surrounds me—everything but the bulbuls
and palm doves gone silent.

Holding still, folding into leafy shade,
I—like the bulbuls—fill myself again
with the breath of leaves,
all that sustains me.

Little Tern

If you could poise
in mid-air—vibrate
your wings just so
        to uplift, depress
        your short-forked tail
        rudder-like, then close
wings and plummet
into the sea's high tide
straight and quick as
        Little tern . . .
        if you could hover
        above the azure waters,
then slice sharp as a knife
through the surface,
then surely you could
        step aside from all thinking,
        and the world would
        be your oyster. It would be
like that fire raging
in your hair—the one Zen
master Deshimaru spoke of—
        consecrating yourself
        completely to each moment.
        Between sky and sea,
the gray-mantled Little tern
living its life—lifting, not
with malice, the unsuspecting
        mollusk or crab from its work-
        a-day world. But listen:
        hear the crab cry of separation,
the mollusk call out,
I am parted from my source.
Now become the delicate tern
        and learn to fly.
        The water is dazzling,
        yet the sky . . .

Dive straight and quick,
then surface and rise up from
the waters like a gleaming
        prayer of thanksgiving.
        On second thought,
        become the mollusk
that got away, and stay always in your
somnolent, seldom turbulent sea.

Aggression, a History Lesson

One Collared dove swoops down,
commences to lord it over the more jovial
Palm doves, interrupting their communal
meal of seeds on my windowsill.
        This is no laughing matter—
        crux of it all since the fateful fall.

And yet in spite of it, a miracle here,
a miracle there—as commonplace once
you begin to expect them as shooting stars
and rainbows: the dog who adopts
        the abandoned kitten, nothing short
        of transcendent mystery. Who knows

how many go unnoticed just because of
disbelief? Miracle enough that Earth goes on
clinging to the Milky Way. But back
to aggression. How something could begin
        so innocently—the Prophet Mohammad
        contending that Arabs on the civilized world's

fringe were overdue their own revelation,
never intending to give rise to a supremist
attitude, which in turn would spark conquest
and dominion. The warrior politician had spoken,
        sparking a revolutionary dynamism—Arab
        expansionism, fragmentation, diversity.

Riven by internal dissent, enduring split between
Sunni and Shi'ite Muslims. External enmity:
medieval Christian Crusades, Mongol invasions,
European imperial increase, the West's thirst for oil.
        I stand at my kitchen sink, shaking my head while
        Laughing doves flee, leaving the bully Collared

to feast alone. In the silence, a bee's drone,
the shifting of barchan dunes, the muezzin's call
to prayer, sirens of an ambulance rushing
        to the latest crash scene—no doubt two men bent
        on lording it over each other in a round-about.

At the Edge of the Arabian Sea,

on a striped mullet skin mat,
sat an old Arab man thin
as a shrunken water-skin,
tossing crumbs to Slender-billed gulls.
        A kingfisher flashed by—
        cobalt blue against gray sky.

November. The air smelled
of fish. Sky promised rain.
        Young women and men passed by—
        eyes, ears glued to mobile phones.

The old man, now lotus-legged,
turned to reading the Qur'an.
        Just beyond, in a vacant lot,
        ten boys played soccer as a setting sun
burst through clouds, turned tan young
bodies into tapers of light.

Ramadan was at its end.
Watching first him, then them,
I wondered what it takes to be holy,
        how best to nourish one's soul.

Six years later my father,
thin as a shrunken water-skin,
sets out sunflower seeds
for birds on the deck; back inside,
he slides into his La-Z-Boy
        to doze away the day.

I slip away, find the photograph—
young and handsome
in his Marine uniform—
          ponder how best
          to celebrate mortality.

Watching him sleep,
the birds feast.

Red-legged Kittiwakes

Today, Red-legged Kittiwakes two
hundred thousand strong breeding
on a vertiginous island cliff of Pribilof,
off Alaska's west coast—some clinging
and some aloft in the mist and wind—
brought me to my knees again.
Seabirds whirled lovely as a company
of couples waltzing under a June moon,

and I withdrew from all abstractions—
even truth of eco-prophecy and warming
waters to approach the beauty swirling
through mist and clinging to a cliff
of spring one more breeding season
off the Bering Sea. What a source of
refuge from life's miseries. Albert
Schweitzer wrote of two—music and cats.
I write of a third: birds.

World of impermanence, and yet
jubilation—these red-legged gulls.
Is it time for me, like Chiyo-ni, to
shave my head and change my name
to Kittiwake—shake up my life and live
the Way of Haikai, angle my wings
in a buoyant flight, find a sheer cliff to
hang out on, settle into a landscape

churning with danger and beauty?
Not hostile. Absolutely complete—
a place to give myself up to.
Rissa brevirostris, gull whose life
clarifies the space between sky,
sea and cliff-face. Its migration
cause enough for joyful celebration.

Yes, shave my head and spread
my feathers. Live off Yellowfin sole
and Redfish. Sleep among Diamond-
leaf willow, Dwarf fireweed,
Tufted saxifrage—chance at last
to vanish into pure infinity.

For the Birds Near the Arctic Circle

The bird book of Svalbard says one can see
more than twenty species late May
till August here in the archipelago—
these the important biotopes for foraging
waders, ducks and gulls: outflow

of expansive river deltas and other tidal
zones; broad valleys with wet tundra
and pools; vegetated places where snow
melts; bird cliffs for fulmar,
guillemot, kittiwake colonies.

Along the ice edge, seabirds congregate
in great numbers to wait
till breeding regions along fjords
become ice-free. Utter wonder—
migrating birds trusting the ice to melt,

flowers and grasses to sprout
through frozen tundra, trusting
in summer, in their nesting grounds
to be intact. Why do I lack
such faith? Such immense fragility

stirs in me a latent humility.
I have come as a penitent pilgrim.
After daylong drizzle and mist,
the sun at precisely 11:30 p.m.
bursts into my porthole, casting

the term *midnight sun* into pure gold.
Northern fulmars, shearing the water,
follow our ship. One huge wave washes
my porthole pane clean. How to close
the eyes on this sublime scene?

Aye, on the shores of darkness there is light,
And precipices show untrodden green . . .

Blissfully watching, pushing away
melancholy thoughts about the future,
torn between timelessness and time
running out, I finally turn away
from the endless sunny night

but remain cradled in the middle
of icy sea and warming sunbeam.

We Are Not Gods

One extreme event, September 2016,
and the second largest Emperor penguin
colony, Antarctica, collapsed—
most severe El Niño in sixty years,
strong winds and record-low sea ice,
the chicks not yet fledged. This is how close

we are to the edge. July 2018, researchers
announce the world's largest colony of King
penguins on the subantarctic Pig Island has shrunk
by nearly 90% these last three decades.
Jeremiah's words echo in my memory,
The whole land . . . a desolation.

The warming, the sacredness of all things,
the eggs, the fledglings, fire's holy
flame remains beyond awake.
The vividness of a gleaming blue glacier—
the sound of its melting, calving enough
to break the heart as it falls apart.

Melting of the ice shields soon to
accelerate, sea levels continue to rise.
Oh to realize we are not gods.
Too many coral reefs bleached and dying.
Dead zones spreading like a cancer
in the oceans. Marine defaunation.

Not like falcons of the Hyperborean cliffs,
nesting far above the sea in a show of audacity
and stamina, vulnerable penguins cannot
climb cliffs as high winds whip across the ice.
Still, a ray of hope: many of those Emperors
moved themselves 35 miles to the south,

joining a colony there where penguins
since have increased tenfold. Behold,
we are not gods. What if it's already
too late? Which is why I wake
at dawn, frightened by the dream,
the cliff edge, the falling.

Vulturine Guineafowl

The new findings made my day—
made me want to shout and howl
Hallelujah! Even the Vulturine guineafowl—
small-brained birds—belong to a complex,
multilevel society and move through
their landscape cohesively with their group.

From a dinosaur-like ancient lineage,
they've evolved a social system
more similar to primates than
other birds. Boldly plumaged
black and blue, bald-headed,
they stroll across the African savanna
in packs, sometimes fighting,
sometimes sharing turf and snacks.

Sound familiar? Groups within groups,
clusters of friends. It made my day
to hear an ornithologist say he suspects
this species is not unique—many more birds
and animals with less than impressive brains
may possess many-layered societies.

What more will it take for humans
to shake the notion we are superior?
I join a mob of red-eyed immense birds
moving across a sweet-scented grassland
past acacias and jackalberries to a marsh,
wishing I knew them each by name—
not one of them the same. Networks
of families and friendships.

They and we are trailing a train
of grazing elephants, the guineafowl
grateful for insects stirred up by them.
And I, driven out of Eden and alone,
        am envious.

I pray the free seeds will have their way—
that Monsanto will never reach this African
grassland where birds, linked by something
hidden and tough as spider silk strands,
understand more than we will ever know.

Holy Sparks

There are holy sparks in all created beings. ~ Thomas Merton

Awakened early by two Palm doves
debating the possibility of mating
on the railing of my bedroom balcony,
I'm listening for dawn breezes.

The cat eases herself up
to the glass to watch, and I witness
holy sparks on both sides—
the doves, the cat. The earth

is shifting, lifting
me up out of winter doldrums,
days lengthening a debatable
mere minute day by January day.

Today I will savor the flavor
of this season, sitting by the window
in the sun, expressing my devotion
to it, taking my place

in the liturgy of the cosmos.
Sleeping and rising alone now,
safe here in my little haven
of a parched desert—no sign

of the usual seasonal winter rains.
I try not to complain, other places
suffering wildfires and hurricanes,
floods and volcanic eruptions.

So many wracked with pain,
loss, grief. I retreat
back to my balcony of tile
and concrete where I can focus

on one bulbul fluffing his plumage
to attract a mate. Together we wait,
palms upturned, arms outstretched,
the cat at my feet slipping back into sleep.

The bulbul in his far from dull
surroundings patiently watches
me watch him in this holy world
beyond that one destroying itself

with noise and too much
busyness—too much movement
and accomplishment.
And all for what?

Another fluff,
and the sparks fly.

Keeping Silent

Within the silence,
  a song. Beneath the frozen
surface of the pond, waters
  warmed by earth's fiery core.

You probe the mountain's
  heart, cut into by a road,
left bleeding. The white
  stork refusing to migrate,

the plum tree to bloom.
  Empty and vulnerable,
abandoned in darkness.
  Hopeless, numbed by loss.

The river too shallow,
  refusing to receive you.
But the reeds speak.
  You keep silent and listen,

heed their warning till by
  morning one ray of light
shatters your dark night.
  Still the dragons and killer sheep

keep you on your toes.
  You watch the cormorant
dive and resurface time and time
  again, follow its shadow under

dark waters, watch as it comes up
  more times than not
empty-beaked. You keep
  your wits about you as you

brood over the void, finally
  resolve to reach continually
for the light—the one you carried
  with you when you entered

this world, determine not
  to be deceived by shadows
and mist, waters too swift
  for the dark swan.

II

Clinging

Barnacles with feathery appendages
gracing the breakwater's rocks—scraping
off algae for sustenance, clinging.

Kneel down. Lean into their world.
But don't touch. Let their silence
and the incoming tide's spray wash

over you till, cleansed of every last
nagging frenzied thought, you become
one of them. But beware: resist the urge

to interfere when the terns and gulls come
to call. Be in their world—become one
of them firmly attached to this Brace Cove

beside the Atlantic Ocean, but bury along
the rocky shore any notion of rewriting
the rules. When the surf lays a sea walnut

at your feet, gently lift it from the wet sand,
hold it in the palm of your hand as if
it is all that exists: gift from the ocean

stretching out before you—standing
between you and Sagres. Call
of the Black-backed gull breaking

the great silence. Brute strength
of marine crustaceans with their fixations
on rocks, whales, hulls of fishing boats

through every season's wind and storm,
breaking the chains of dominance
that have bound you too long.

Finally ask yourself: would you be
the thunderbird creating storms,
or the barnacle clinging?

Envisioning Mercy

Mercy shall not be for man alone,
but shall go beyond and embrace the whole world.
~ Swami Vivekananda

The elephant with severe arthritis
is forced to perform,
its owner blind to her pain,
deaf to her moans.

Feel for a human pulse
within the phenomenal world's
workings. Stand
at the still point of darkness:

observe Earth hanging
by a thread. Gandhi once said
you can judge a society's morality
by how it treats its animals.

Once, I swayed for nearly half a day
on an elephant's shoulders.
Arrived sunset, Karen village
deep in Thailand's jungle.

When the harness was removed,
and I saw the raw groove
rubbed by the friction of it against hide,
I cried. There were tears, as well,

in the old elephant's eyes.
Lying awake that night
on the floor of my host's hut,
I wondered what the elephant was up

to, tied just outside the door,
taken so many years before
from her family. Lonely,
          solitary.

If I could have,
I would have taken her
into my arms and rocked her
all night long, wiping the tears

from her eyes, the ooze
from her weeping side's
wound. If she was up to it,
I would have stolen her away,

ushered her back to the scene
of the crime, searched high and low
till we could find her family.
Feel for a human pulse.

Stand at the still point
of darkness. Imagine
what lies beyond pain
and starkness. Dare ask

the question yet again,
What will you gain,
though you rule the world,
if you lose your soul?

Anatomy of Empathy

For seven long years in South Korea,
at Yongin's Everland Zoo, Koshik lived alone—
another victim of human acquisitiveness.

They say this Asian elephant
construed a way of speaking
the language of his keepers

by sticking his trunk into his mouth
and tongue-shaping plosive trumpetings
into intelligible Korean words.

If this does not stir your heart
to compassion, nothing will.
Have you heard of Julius,

living in Lindner's sanctuary
for homeless parrots—afraid
of the others because he doesn't think

he is one? If only his owner had tried
to be nature instead of mere man.
If instead he had entered the terrain

of Julius' ancestral domain without
disturbing the grass. Treat each parrot,
each elephant as highly intelligent,

sacred gift from the Creator.
Look into the eyes of one terrorized
by bullhook and electric prod.

See the light of God brimming
from her soul. Enter the mosque,
the temple, the cathedral. Feel

beheld and uplifted by just one elephant,
one parrot—you'll never be the same.
Is it too late for me to change

professions? Study anthrozoology?
Comfort, soothe, smooth out ruffled
feathers, remove the harness and chains,

apply the salve to hides rubbed raw,
to puncture wounds and lacerations,
share their pain of separation, torn from

clan and native land? I would give them
back their roiling creeks, swaying grasses,
damp woods, real tree branches

in place of artificial perching posts.
To hold in my palm or arms
the old and transcendent too long

out of their element—each of us
moving the other beyond
the aftermath of trauma.

Ray of Darkness

Three years now since he died,
another spring has arrived.
I've tried to be as nonattached
as the frog rising to the surface,
    to be as equally balanced
    between light and dark
    as the Vernal Equinox.

Species are declining
at an accelerating rate,
    the culprit of this Sixth
Extinction man—culminating
product of the Cenozoic Era.

We choose to ease
our consciences with zoos
and wildlife sanctuaries,
and pen the finest obituaries
for those we lose.

A year now since Sudan died—
the last male northern white
rhino, and I have tried to go
on living with hope. How else
to survive these final years but
to keep alive my faith that a few
will always do enough good to
            counter the evil.

Today's good news: they think
one species presumed extinct—
    Formosan clouded leopard—
may in fact still be roaming its
lowland forest of southern Taiwan.

Faith is nothing more nor less
than a ray of darkness, but a lot less
bleak than doubt.

Camels Going to Market

In the bed of a Toyota truck,
they ride, looking dignified—
        nonchalant and unconcerned
        as cars and lorries on all sides churn,

some speeding past, some tail-gating.
Their eyes, long double-lashed, ask
        What's the rush? Why not try waiting
        your turn, this lovely autumn morning?

I've watched them unbridled,
        grazing the rodat, or stretched out
in close proximity to their beloved
        Ziziphus nummularia,

        lazing away the hot midday.
Calmly one gazes my way,
demanding respect. I would protect
        all three from the day's ordeal.

No doubt they've served their masters well.
        One rises slowly, sinuously
        from its sitting position, hinting
                of growing dissent, no menace

in her eyes—only a dispassionate gaze
        void of fear or trepidation
        as she moves nearer her destination.
                Camels so full of grace,

                heading to the marketplace,
        my heart grieved to see them come
        to this sad plight. Yet I take note:
                each one's *appareled in celestial light.*

If Only

. . . truth brings joyous tranquility. ~ Rumi

Bedtime, I turn out the light,
open the window to find a doe
and her twin fawns lounging
on the lawn, the calm spirit
of nature stretched out before me,

sweet and soft as a lullaby.
For a moment, I forget
the vole's cry as the owl
snatched it up at dusk,
forget all the day's bad news—

latest tally of what we're poised
to lose, the latest mass shootings
El Paso and Dayton—forget
heaven's pull, and content
myself with the lull of what's right

here within reach—the white-
tailed deer. An orphan now,
feeling homeless here till this
mother and her spotted twins
draw me in to their warmth.

If only I could shapeshift and sit
with them all night on the cool grass
beside the birdbath, under the stars.
Or be invisible and silently settle
beside them, becoming one with my kin.

Territorial Disputes

Now my pacifism's put to the test.
Bully cat's gone too far, bit the timid
tom so hard its backside needs suturing—
a nearly two-hundred-dollar vet bill.
Heard myself threatening to kill.
Always it comes down to this:

territorial disputes. The Gaza Strip today.
The Everglades yesterday. And the day before,
Asian man pushed to his northeastern limits,
following after a wounded mammoth.
Kotzebue Sound, Mackenzie south
to Saskatchewan, the American plains,

finally Florida to live along the St. Johns.
1492 Columbus sailing west to possess by flag,
sword, cross the Bahamas and other islands.
And from that point on, an endless throng
of discoverers, adventurers, conquerors.
Island after island of Indians, eventually

even those fiercest ones, of the 'Glades.
Say you kill the bully. Return
the timid one, stitches removed,
to the garden. How long before the next
bully appears? Try hard to disregard
the possibility. Ignore the shadow

creeping along the wall. Think positive.
Imagine no hunger, *nothing to kill or*
die for in the garden, the timid cat lounging
in afternoon sun, too lethargic to chase
off bulbuls and sparrows or gobble up
grasshoppers, its purring God's reassuring

all shall be well. But remember the sad
histories—aborigines and so many lost
species, greed the enemy. Not hunger.
I give the bully his own bowl—keep it full
to overflowing, but still he attacks
the timid tom. What can I say?

Watching Zebras and Doves

Northern end near the pyramid-
shaped Sheraton, a small population
of Zebra doves resides and breeds,
getting everything they need
from gardens and grounds

around the hotel. Most likely
descendants of escaped caged birds,
fending for themselves now,
seeking out seeds and insects.
Geopelia striata from Southeast Asia—

slender, black and white on brown
upperparts. Watching them, taking
my time, Africa still on my mind,
I recall the Burchell's zebras,
observed just days ago grazing

the savanna, and doves—
Red-eyed, Laughing, Emerald-
spotted, Wood, Cape Turtle,
African Mourning adorning
the bush with grace.

Watching zebras and doves,
one begins to believe again,
to understand why the ancients
worshipped animals and birds.
These gentle ones hurt no one,

take only enough to subsist,
are neither greedy nor needy,
ask nothing of anyone. Oh,
to approach the world with such
non-aggression and clear vision.

Empty

All the frenzied madness
going on around me, the sadness,
I try harder than ever to be empty—

like the space between the spokes
of a hub, the inside of a bathtub.
Empty so I might be useful,

so the reality sinks in: an elephant
is killed for his or her tusks every
fifteen minutes—slaughtered,

body left to rot like all those bison
years ago on the American plains.
Empty so there's room to grieve,

to forgive,
to love.
Empty

so the poetics of faith
might wash over me,
and I might live in God's mercy.

Empty
so when I come face
to face with the owl—

his legs dangling over my lawn
on his nightly prowl—
I can be drawn into his world,

make time and space
for our communion,
for mercy and grace.

III

Since Svalbard's Discovery,

1596, human activities have been
these: hunting and fishing, coal
mining, tourism, research
and education. Conservation
and protection now in vogue,

the veil between us and them
thinning—sixty-five per cent
of the land, seventy per cent
of territorial waters now bird
sanctuaries, national parks,

nature reserves. How absurd
it now seems—all the exploitation
of whales, walruses, seals
and bears. Who cares
to wear real fur these days?

Or corsets and parasols
ribbed by baleen? Obscene!
But as for those tusks of the walrus
and narwhal gone missing,
one might ask the Chinese

what's up their sleeves
(dietary therapy?) and guard closely
the small island of Moffen.
After four hundred years
of exploitation—wintertime

trapping of fox and polar bear,
springtime sealing, summer
bird-catching and collecting
of down and eggs, autumn hunting
of reindeer and ptarmigan—

I hear myself praying again
with earnestness Eliot's
prayer, *Teach us to care*
and not to care,
Teach us to sit still.

Orvieto, or Another Way to Pray

In Italy, I made a point to visit
that hill town poised on a flat summit
of a volcanic tuff's butte because I
wanted to know intimately the place where
grapes grow for my favorite white wine—
        fruity and floral, with a hint of pears.
        I threw away all cares that day, taking
        my time to watch grapes ripen on the vine—
        felt more a part of this earth
        than I had for a long long time.

Born in sync with the stars, grains of sand,
quails and vines of grape, I settled in to wait
among ripening grapes to escape the world eaters
who, in the end, are devoured by their own frenzy.
        Silent and still, bones softening,
        I became a grape. Yes, I shape-
        shifted and found myself lifted up, a bit
        like floating on air currents, like I once did
        when I rowed on feathers over the sea
        with gulls. Yes, it was just like floating
        as the sun's warmth filled me. No longer
        was nature a stranger, though I must confess
        I know her less than I would like to,
        no matter how close I get.

Still, when I pressed my ear to the vine,
I heard less of my own voice and more
of the sublime. No longer was there
a need to ask who caused the grapevine
to rise up out of Umbrian soil, who arranged
the precise delivery of sun and rain,
warmth and aridity. Among the growing
grapes that day, I learned another way to pray,

kneeling down between two rows.
Felt blessed, caressed by tufaceous soils
and the Paglia no less than the grapes themselves—
Procanico and Grechetto,
Drupeggio and Malvasia Toscana.

Yes, I felt blessed, and I gave thanks
for the ones who had taken time—labored
in love—to dress each and every vine.

On the Feast Day of St. Clare

On the Feast of St. Clare,
I pause to remember
when I was there,
walking the cobbled streets
of her town Assisi,

where living appeared unhurried
and easy. I made a vow
then and there that somehow
I'd find a way to tread day by day
gently on this earth, in harmony

with all species, taking only
my share—perhaps even less
than that—giving back
what I don't need to subsist,
walking softly, deliberately,

paying rapt attention to birds
and feral cats, weeds and all
unwanted beings with special needs,
saving seeds to keep me ever
mindful of life's fragile

sacredness, writing haiku
in order to pursue the essence,
letting go the dream of owning
a sailboat with decks of teak
and a mast of Sitka spruce,

weaving together science
and beauty with cattails,
blue silt and star dust.
I made a vow
so many years ago now

in Assisi—it clings to me
like sand forming a dune
in a desert, taking its stand
with impermanence
against extravagance.

Twelve Days in the Tongass,

immersed in the wild,
wet wilderness, as precious
a paradise as one might ever know,
as fine a line to tow
between world's vacuity
and reality as one might choose.

The Pacific living up to its name,
flowing through fjords,
        past mellow meadows where
        Black and Brown bears lounge
        away the days waiting
        for the salmon to return,

creation and destruction going hand
in hand so one can finally understand
and trust the dance, balance quite well
        between avalanche and glacial moraine,
        between Milky Way's light and dark—
                within the still point of light's energy.

Here, in the Tongass,
it becomes clear: everything
merits deliverance—
        no creature, tree, rock, salmon
        caught making its way upstream
        to spawn deserving of suffering.

Arctic Kidney lichen colonizing old snags,
decaying trunks, red bones of cedars.
        The loon's cry of grief or joy
        closing the gap between lake and sky.
                Gulls hurling keep away calls
                or *hallelujahs* at intruders.

Twelve days in the Tongass'
dripping, pouring, splashing world
where steep, granite walls glisten
as mountain goats sip mist, and
drenched ferns enlist the heart in
intercession for all the wildlife here.

Everglades History Lesson One

First the Calusas, Mayaimis,
Tekestas came—living on fish and game,
fashioning tools out of seashells.

Then Spanish Conquistadors—
and Tekestas, Mayaimis were no more.
Only Calusas, scattered, remained.
But the Spaniards didn't stay—
frightened away by razor-sharp ridged
sedge and bellowing alligators.

Next, the Creeks—Muskogee-
speaking people from the west—
and Seminoles, kicked out of
the Carolinas by European invaders.

Then white hunters annihilating two million
egrets and Roseate spoonbills for breeding
feathers to adorn women's hats, killing
alligators for hides to craft shoes and wallets.

Then engineers digging canals, draining
fresh water to make farmland and towns.

Finally pesticides, fertilizers flowing
into the waters, poisoning one-celled
animals, snails, mammals, fish,
birds and plants. Doesn't everyone wish

for a happy ending? Endangered ecosystem
restored to its splendor? Swamp lily,
Calopogon orchid thriving? Crocodile,
Liguus tree snail, Green anole surviving
to extol the Everglades' glory—its central
solitudes holding fast time's secrets?

Doesn't everyone hope beyond all
hope Jeremiah heard wrong?

Returning

> *We are nature, long have we been absent,*
> *but now we return.*
> ~ Walt Whitman

Never to be quite the same, I came
to the Everglades. Once one has
walked alone at dusk among alligators,
how to ever again content oneself
among one's own species? Once
Meister Eckhart's words sink in,

as they will when you linger with one
Roseate spoonbill, *Nothing in all*
creation is so like God as stillness,
how to resume a safe speed?
Hushed by harmonies of Little Grass,
Green and Cricket frogs, stopped

in one's tracks by Soft-shelled turtles
nibbling on Spatterdock leaves and
Pond apples, consoled along footpaths
and boardwalks through mangroves and those
hardwood hammocks harboring the last
of the great mahoganies, one senses

an eternal recompense, a peace
both cause and goal of creation—
Everglades made of primordial love.
But then the ships came in—
hauled away egrets' and spoonbills'
plumes. Fledglings left to starve,

whole rookeries decimated.
As pilgrim kneeling where a game
warden was murdered protecting them,
Indians enslaved and slaughtered,
Jesuit priests martyred, I return,
am nature now, and I grieve.

Fire Raging, Questions Blazing

> *Live the questions now. Perhaps, then, someday far into the future, you will gradually, without even noticing it, live your way into the answer.*
>
> ~ Rainer Maria Rilke

A fire raging in my hair,
I *live the questions now* as best
I dare, though I admit I do at times
attempt to answer them.

But I can trust Rilke was right
when Harvest Moon beams on wild
asters in bloom, and light and dark
present themselves in equal balance,

when I taste summer in apple and chestnut,
perceive maple leaves becoming all fire
and the full moon cooling every lingering,
niggling desire—filling me

with compassion, when I refuse
to turn away, living the questions today
though bits of shrapnel lodge
in my skin, and I'm torn between

pop culture and politics,
saints and heretics, when I whirl
in my white robe in the company
of gulls and ghosts along the deserted

Inland Sea's coast, when I finally believe
with my whole heart this is all I need—
little dot of a desert with its rapt light
delineating a thousand shades of tan,

brown, white—when camels,
earth spirits and wildflowers become
my mentors, fire raging, questions blazing,
no end to the suffering, the dunes

continually shifting, hamadas and gravel
plains cracking, White-cheeked bulbuls
flashing yellow vents like glints of gold
as they flush out insects and moths

from the lofts of desert scrub.
Fire raging, living the question:
What in God's name
could it possibly be for—

this latest insane war?
My neighbors just back from
their country, Iraq—telling
the horrors, eyes full of sorrow.

And I, from Cambodia—
landmines still claiming limbs,
mosquitoes lives. Fire raging
in my hair, I would live spare—

spin Khmer silk in a room
small and bare. Living
the questions—this world,
the next—each question mark

a glimmer of hope, pinprick
dispelling the dark, each one
a likely key to unlock the deepest,
most guarded answer.

Imbolic (Candlemas) Day

Halfway there now, the light
returning, my soul begins yearning
for the soul of nature, giver
of all life. With reverence
and humility, I seek to know
the Mystery, close my door
on the chaos to compose haiku
and a five-bu candlestick, all
the while wishing I were brazen
enough to scrawl graffiti across
a government wall, like those brave
young Syrians stirring an uprising.

Halfway there now, I'm sensing
all life stirring Denali to Death Valley,
Siberia to Arabia, along the flyways
and ancient migratory routes
land and sea—every single creature
loved by me. The light returning,
I spend my days discerning
poems the shamal scrawls across
the desert, whirling to the rhythm
of the scant rains' refrain.

At night, halfway there now,
after the day's lengthening light,
I settle into the nebulous dark
and wait for questions of faith,
the revelations, to come—
swayed this is no time now
to succumb to doubt or fear.

We are almost there.

IV

Beyond All Hunger and Ambition

Do you not feel it—
a collective holding of our breaths
waiting for the next mass shooting
suicide bombing natural disaster
now that they're coming more often,
        the latest shooting reminding me
        why I keep refusing to check email frequently
        throughout the day. I stay as far away
        from the persistent bombardment as I can.
My mind and heart cannot stand
constant reminders of what we humans
are capable of, how little progress
we've made toward love.

But memories haunt me,
always hovering in the shadows:
        Cambodia's killing fields, the Holocaust,
        Tibetans' sixty-year existence under
        Chinese dominance, women considered
        witches burned at the stake—and Giordano
        Bruno because he wouldn't back down—
                believed Earth did go round the sun,
                and the universe was infinite.

Do you not smell them—
    bodies burning, turning into ash
    high up on the world's rooftop?

Do you ever stop and wonder why
we cannot break this cycle of evil?
Why we will not
        surrender to Earth's intelligence
            so we can *rise up rooted like trees*?

Let the rarefied breeze set to motion
the colorful *lunga* prayer flags
on Tibet's mountaintops, spreading
peaceful wishes out over the world.
          Let everything at last—
          steel, concrete, glass—
return to dust as everything must,
to end in the sacred wind.

Do you not see it—
beyond the muddy, silted river—
          hear it: the flash of light,
          hum of life that if placed on your
tongue like a Communion wafer
would dissolve all doubt and fear.

Try to see completely just one
relict species—the Crab-plover.
Let it bowl you over, this last survivor
of a group now gone extinct.
          Its long pale blue legs tempering
          sand spits and intertidal flats.
Watch it stab a mollusk or crab,
then break it up by pounding it to death,
same as any human chef, taking one
          life to sustain another.

Do you not sense it—long
for it—that place beyond
all hunger and ambition,
          filled with grace?

Subhanallah

When Muslims encounter God's miracles in or through nature, they whisper this Arabic word.

If you complain the desert is drab,
I'll know you've never watched it
transform under the sunset's glow.

If you insist heaven is a place above
and beyond, I'll know you have yet to open
your eyes and ears to what's right here—

gods dwelling among us—have yet
to reverse the belief that the species *Homo*
sapiens is the center of the universe.

If you wail all is ugly and broken,
I'll know you have failed to go
into the service of beauty—to yield

to curiosity and the mystery
of the god within, the divinity
of Earth herself, to spend

a night on a forest floor in the sight
of bears and owls, to awaken to the call
of birds and the warmth of the rising sun.

If you decide you're done, there's nothing
more to live for, I'll know it's time
to take you by the hand and guide you

to the seashore or riverbank where you can
witness both heron and fish thanking their lucky
stars to be alive right where they are.

In Between Haram *and* Halal

are three shades in the middle:
makrouh—offensive, something not
liked at all; *mashbooh*—quite doubtful;
and *mushtabahat*—questionable.

These three are quite tricky, causing
I dare say most of the problems,
making a strong case against black
and white. Only three things

will help you do right: the blessing
of light within and without—in
your heart, on your skin; blessing
of rain; blessing of earth.

Three shades in the middle
between permissible and not.
The glaciers are melting.
Is it too late

to do an atom's weight
of good, to read the book
of Creation? let each leaf
of the tree become a page of scripture?

The trick is to balance between soul
and stone, to roam between seashore
and desert dunes. Three shades
in the middle. This is more than a riddle:

Say your work horse grows old.
You buy a tractor to replace him. Do you
turn him out into the field to graze away
his last days, or sell him as dog meat?

The leaves' veins are parched.
Dust is all that fills the cup.
Three shades. Can you hear the rain
coming? Polar ice pack breaking apart?

Three shades. To catch fish just
for the pleasure of it, then throw them
back in, believing they feel no pain
from their hook-torn bleeding mouths?

This is about the day-to-day mundane—
the wide gray expanse
in between *haram* and *halal*—
your last chance to get it right.

Teaching Anthropocene Children

With time running out,
children need only to learn about
this: All life is one; humans
are not on the top rung—
for sure, not the measure
of all things.

We must teach them
how to listen, watch and see
each and every species for *who*
not *what* they are in all
their uniqueness and complexity.

What children need to learn
these days is all the animals,
birds and fish can teach—to reach
beyond the violence and grief
to the peace of wild things,
to let the carpet of russet
leaves in autumn fill them not
with regret but with courage to
accept life and death.

What children need to learn
these last days is how to discern
the word of the Creator in each creature,
how to practice a little faith,
how to wait in darkness like seeds
germinating under the ground,
how to listen for the sound
of rebirth beyond death.

Nature's Revered Teachers

> *The old pine tree teaches wisdom,*
> *and the cry of the wild bird expresses truth.*
> ~ Zen koan

The silent stone—
how it lectures on the sacredness
of stillness and muteness.
        The Pleistocene,
        time of great extinctions,
        teaches mystery and curiosity—

was it a star dragon
thrusting out its tongue,
or the heat of meteoritic impact?
        Meltwater teaches chemistry
        and tragedy, and most important
        perhaps these days, humility.

The blushing peach—
what a wordless lesson
it can teach.
        The fire, tempering the sword,
        clarifies how we, too, require softening
        if we are to resist breaking.

The owl, turning its head
160 degrees, exemplifies that being
anticipatory is only half the story.
        La Venta and San Lorenzo,
        southern Mexico, from
        whose ground colossal stone heads

of the lost Olmec culture
were unearthed, teach the ghostly
hush of vanishment.
          Windborne swirls of silvery seeds
          suggest that man also has the need
          to launch off to new worlds.

And the poisoned dying bee,
in perfect stillness, teaches eternity—
takes us back to the Book of Romans,

          all creation groaning for salvation.

These Days

These days it's the insignificant
holds me spell-bound.
It's those who do not talk

I listen to. I no longer
chase after money and success.
Instead, I traipse after butterflies

through toxic flowerless
meadows. And I've let go
all strivings for perfection.

Now I'm given to accepting
myself and everything as is.
These days I'm into waiting for—

not possessing/grasping—God,
and bonding with other species
(each one a Word from the Creator),

rising above questions of truth
and falsity, allowing the thrush
high up in treetops to remain

elusive and ambiguous.
These days I chant, not the hundred
names of God, but the names of

towns and prisons poisoned by oil
and chemical industries. I count
the earthquakes set off by hydro-

fracking. I'm tracking
what we've gained,
all we're lacking,

and I give myself to believing
eternity is the ultimate
escape from modernity.

The Secret to Positive Thinking

> *All shall be well, and all shall be well,*
> *and all manner of thing(s) shall be well.*
> ~ Julian of Norwich

Even if I could consistently believe
Julian's words, I still would save
seeds—life's fragile sacredness
I'd still guard and respect.

And though I believe,
I would still grieve for skylarks,
song thrushes, blackbirds gone silent—
their marshes, moors and meadows,

ponds, heaths and hedgerows poisoned—
destroying their food supply.
Though I believe, I would still cry
out against *a strange passivity*

haunt(ing) our lives. I would despise
all homogenized shrinking of the world,
dwindling of personalities,
dulling of relationship.

I would not slight the little spore
that blights the potato, the one small spark
that ignites the forest. All shall be well,
regardless of what befell

the world yesterday. If I can say this
and believe it, the battle's won.
Look how the Black-capped chickadees
have fun in their forest, flitting about

collectively, each respectively
doing its thing. Silent and weightless,
harmless, disturbing neither limb
nor air, alert to all that goes there.

Surely they believe all shall be well.
How else could they be so full of grace—
the very face of God, each one the sum
total of perfection? All shall be well.

Just ask the river otters, frolicking in brown
waters, tummy-up, holding out both hands.
But—ah, the curse of man, always a but—
what about the bees, their hives

no longer humming? I cannot
ignore the disaster coming.
          Dare I still believe
          all shall be well?

In Search of My Own Hazelnut

Oh for the faith of Julian
holding that small round thing,
size of a hazelnut, all that is made,
believing it shall last because
God made, loves and keeps it.

Was there no species extinction
in her day, or did she simply turn away?

Today the loss and brokenness is too
much, humans having wandered far
from the sacred way.

Tonight, when the Harvest Moon
rises full and bright, I shall walk
the desert floor cracked and dry
as always before the first autumn
rains. And casting eyes moonward,
my vision refreshed, I shall find
something small and round to lift up
from the parched cracked ground—
                    perhaps a fossil sea urchin—
to hold and believe like Julian it shall
last, no questions asked,
beyond this time of terror.

But just now, late morning, I look
into the mirror to meet eyes looking
out—staring back at me—with doubt.

Still, let me keep all day before me
the leitmotif of the unflinching
faithful believer bowing to the infinite
Maker and Keeper.

To Life

May what I do flow from me like a river,
no forcing and no holding back,
the way it is with children.
~ Rainer M. Rilke

To realize—to tap into—
that direct line to the divine.

To reverence creation—
make of each new sunrise
a celebration.

To let being not doing
be my priority,
make silence my preference.

To be filled with *ruthless*
compassion, ears perceptive
to suffering cries,
yet practice the peace
of detachment.

To leave the weeds—
dandelions, mustard,
goldenrod—for the bees.

To bless, as St. Francis did
the sow, each creature
I'm honored to know.

To see with my heart
the invisible, believe
the unbelievable.

So much can go wrong—
to sing a song of thanksgiving
for all that is right.

To take time to arrange
flowers in a vase,
fruit on the windowsill.

To keep still or crawl slowly
with the snail in spite of
the world's ceaseless spinning.

To make losing my goal—
money, possessions, obsessions—
finally realizing cashing in's
not all it's cracked up to be.

To be able, finally,
to say with acknowledgment
and full acceptance,

C'est la vie!

Released into the Light

The wound is the place where the light enters you. ~ Rumi

One yellow bougainvillea leaf
    is freed by the brief visitation
of a Laughing dove preoccupied
    with his lifelong chosen mate.
Hours have passed since the break
    of day, dusk still so far away.
Gradually the canopy's anatomy
    looms clear, and one cocks an ear

to hear above senseless human chatter
    the only message to matter—
plangent calling of wild geese.
    Sitting in autumn sun and wind,
you wait—anticipate
    the hesitant moon, the dark night
when thoughts take flight,
    and no longer a mere parasite

on this earth, you roam among
    the stars. Released
into the light that enters you,
    you become free. The wound
closes as you lift your eyes and drift
    among stars, not at all surprised
to realize finally who and where
    you are—starlight so bright

you're nearly blinded after eons
    of dark night. Now death itself
is buried deep and cannot keep
    its appointment with you.
Light shooting through every
    vein and artery, you've broken
open, like a water lily
    over its dark pond.

Enduring Burning

> *What is to give light must endure burning.* ~ Viktor Frankl

Take Prometheus,
giving the gift of fire to lift
man up out of the dark mire,
then bound by great chains
to a mountain peak where all
he could do was shriek
in torment as, burning,
vultures ate his liver.

Take meteoroids showering
their light across a dark night,
then vaporizing out forever.

And that yellow dwarf, the sun—
day after day burning all that Hydrogen
till it's used up, then to continue
for another 130 million years
to burn Helium, expanding till it
engulfs Mercury, Venus, Earth
to become a red giant,
finally to collapse into a white
dwarf, but for now enduring,
giving light to the blazing

corn poppies, who, too,
endure burning to give light
to the passing pilgrims en route
to Santiago de Compostela.

And so it goes on—each field,
each pond, everything taking on
the task of enduring burning,

giving light to triumph
over eons of dark night.

V

Feast of St. Brigit

Perhaps if I hadn't grown up reading
the *Holy Bible* since age seven,
believing I wouldn't go to heaven
unless I *hurt not the earth,*

neither the sea nor the trees,
I wouldn't feel so deeply
my connection, my duty,
my need for nature.

Now the movement of life
from winter to spring,
the rebirth of everything—
all of earth waking as from

a deep sleep—stirs in me
a need for bonding with every
species. Though I'm pledged
to detachment, I sense the sacrament

of oneness with all things being
born. And yet, to accept death—
to experience the elegance
of absence. How can this be,

this feeling of connection while
practicing detachment? Growing
old now, I become apocalyptic,
bent on warning. But let me keep

my will to feel empathy for both
my human and nonhuman kin.
I would do it all again—read
the Good Book beginning to end,

trust in resurrection—the dead
dried flowers offering their seeds
once the rains come, and vow
never to hurt a single earthly species.

No Death

> *The smallest sprout shows there is really no death.*
> ~ Walt Whitman, from *Song of Myself*, Section 6

Stuck in a traffic jam
on a Doha street, I seek
relief and find it

in a weed sprouting from a crack
in the median strip pavement.
One continuous, indigenous weed

just what I need
to reassure me all shall be well,
just as Julian of Norwich held.

Instead of ranting with all of my
fellow commuters, I give thanks
for a persistent weed,

enjoy the simple beauty
and audacity (pluck) of a plant
refusing to die.

And so must I,
though this aggressive,
progressive, over-developing city

threatens to pave right over me.
Its slave I will not be.
This little visible weed

revealing the invisible protector
of the weak, the divine power
moving for all time through all

creation. What liberation
these thoughts provide
as I finally drive

on to my destination,
feeling empowered somehow
by a simple sprout. And isn't this

what living's all about—thriving
in the most difficult, unlikely,
inhospitable conditions?

Refusing, till the time comes—
not at one's own bidding—
to lay down one's tired bones?

Which, with any luck, will rise up
(be dug up) to nourish creatures
and cause native flowers to flourish.

I Turn My Face to the Sun

When the day's bad news bombards me,
I turn my face to the sun—my attention
to the victories, like the plummeting
of veal production, thanks to HFA's
relentless media campaigns.

I rejoice with twelve hundred rescued
farm animals living out their days
at Suwanna Ranch. I praise the humans
showing them the face of God. How odd
to focus on the negative

when all around us people
are daring to live courageous lives.
We are all cohabitants of endangered
habitats—victims of imminent forces
of chaos. Yet to move beyond

the malaise of soul and celebrate
the victories, accept consequences.
The thing is not to forget,
though remembering may lay
us low. Still, the point is to know

we are not innocent, and yet dare
to forgive ourselves and turn our faces
to the sun. We are not yet done
for. A bit of summer still remains.
Listen: the cicada refrain

orchestrating the humid air
with persistent intent. Linger
between fading crepe myrtle blossoms
and gliding Tiger Swallowtail
at the buddleia nectar—between

the living and the dying.
Be fully alert to what remains
of the dwindling season.
Let each small marvel be
your reason to go on.

Be like the mockingbird that sings
come rain or shine. Learn something
new about the mundane divine
each day you move through
this wondrous mysterious world.

Nature's Patience

To lose patience is to lose the battle. ~ Mahatma Gandhi

Late summer, my remembrance
of springtime is as incense
to my senses, the thought of energy

withdrawing into the earth
early August for seeds soon to fall
and germinate all winter a lullaby.

I wait in her presence
to learn how to reverence
creation, and in so doing, gain patience—

determine not to hurry,
and so avoid the flurry
of those rushing around me.

Patience, and the rain and change
will come. Patience enough
to speak across the divide,

courageously ask questions,
stand side by side
and make connections.

Patience when it seems all is lost,
it's too late, but still to wait
for the sake of our human,

animal, vegetable siblings.
Patience to wade through
the scientific evidence,

political maneuverings
(shenanigans) of industrialized
(despised) societies.

Patience to reimagine,
though spring has grown more silent,
its suffering more profound.

Patience enough to reflect back
to that *once upon a time*
and forward to the day of final victory.

Patience, like that
honed by the goldfinches
waiting all summer

for thistles to rise
and the wind disperse
their gifts of seeds.

Indistinguishable

I'm a tad bit
like the Orange Tip—
in day flight quite
conspicuous. But come night,
settled in on a flower head—
wings folded—I blend in
to my background, sound
of jazz, become nearly
          indistinguishable.

No longer pressing myself
into everything—stressing
and obsessing—no longer
devouring, I'm allowing
life to be enough—simply
breathing and being. I become
light, weightless, and in the darkness
mysteriously bright from the radiance
and presence of something(one)
immortal in the portal of silence.
Tranquillité d'esprit. I am free.
No longer in a whirlwind, I blend in.

Alone, I listen to the music of saxophone
or trumpet, and realize there's nowhere
I'd rather be save perhaps in the company
of a family of elephants, with its wise
matriarch like an angel holding all
the knowledge needed for survival.

In the darkness, blending in, I pray
for those who sin against the elephants
and earth, who kill and do irredeemable harm,
and I search for words to trumpet the alarm.

Indistinguishable from the depth,
I hold my breath and wait
in the darkness, longing to hibernate
through the oncoming winter.

After Reading Steps Toward a Small Theory of the Visible *by John Berger*

Frightening me the most
is the global appetite for more—
            that mirage, a ghost into which
            the body, the existent, vanishes.

Who desires to be disembodied?
free of all that is required,
to dwell in unreality,
the virtual, in isolation?

I'd rather remain in the natural domain
of necessity, zoom in with paper
and pen to save things from chaos,
abandon everything else, become

receiver from now until the end,
collaborate and celebrate
each unique created being
as it emerges out of darkness,

be devoted to the existent,
persistent in willingness
to become more receptive,
let my own body intensify

as the appeal and energy
of every other creature enters me.
            Let all transient, virtual things
            around me vanish. I will listen

to each written river, mountain,
flower, bird and remember—carry on
            a dialogue with each one—
in this way elude the deathly solitude,

false images and disembodied
of these times, instigating hope
by writing the existent—
          my final act of resistance.

Hope

Hope stops you in your tracks today—
that lofty ideal with feathers
that perches in the soul,

what St. Francis has commissioned you
to sow in every place where despair
has spread like kudsu or bamboo.

Lofty as love, hope looks at absolute
contradiction—life, death—
and pronounces a benediction.

Hope is a persistent vow
to live in the eternal now.
It hears in the temple bell

the music of the spheres
and knows quite well worldly
success does not equal happiness.

Hope sets out compelling,
exquisite signposts to prospects,
moves beyond fleeting comfort

to shake you out of complacency,
places you firmly, once and for all,
within miracles' gleaming walls.

Hope compiles all possibilities,
hangs on as firmly as the chameleon
with its sticky toe pads.

It doesn't come undone
by the pollution-smeared horizon,
the absence of flamingos who've fled

the chaos of coastal development.
Hope is feather-light, star-bright.
It cannot help itself—ever-optimistic,

shying away from the realistic,
it leans toward the ideal.
It floats above summer's fading

mustard fields like a grasshopper,
depositing its over-wintering eggs
in full faith spring will come again.

To Save Us from the Dark

Every atom is
vibrant with life.
Existing in the smallest
creature is a spirit of fight
to survive. But beyond
the life and fight,
a holy light—a spark
dispelling the dark.

Call the source from which
it ignites whatever you wish—
love, God, Gaia,
Center Galactic Source,
Creator of all Creation,
Great Spirit, Mother, Father.
Holy sparks scattered
by the desert lark's flight,
by bioluminescent plankton
glowing at the shoreline.

Daffodils frilling the greening
hills, whippoorwills calling,
stalling the night's chill.
Holy sparks to counter
the Age of Terror, which would
extinguish all hope if we could not
distinguish between the false
and the holy, the latter preventing
our returning to the Dark Age.
Holy sparks in stardust, which of course
comes down to us—*is* us.

A warbler announcing spring,
doing his holy spark-flinging thing.
A fig tree full of sun-baked soil
and holy sparks within each fruit.
Even in the least-loved ragweed,
the millipede—holy, holy
sparks to save us from the dark.

Come Bask in the Divine Light

If you love everything, you will perceive the divine mystery in things.
~ Dostoyevsky, from *The Brothers Karamazov*

It's so simple really,
and exactly as Dostoyevsky put it.
Practicing it for such a long
time now—loving every tree,
bird, animal, *ray of God's light*—
I'd say he got it so right.

Such a surplus of existence
all around us—bright stars
shining down on devastated land,
carpet of scarlet leaves spread
under bare trees, season of
mists—every thorn bush drips
with moisture, holy
as a cathedral cloister.

If you love everything,
even the diseased elm trees,
you'll plant seeds, defiantly
believing there is hope.

You'll become transparent
among trees, the divine mystery
whispering in winter wind,
green holly, sun's rising
and setting, tides that abide
by the moon's bidding, the tribe
of Tiger, call of an owl on his
nightly prowl, finches perched
on apple branches, two bulbuls
exchanging devoted glances.

Yes, you'll take your chances
on loving everything, though the more
you love, the more you'll lose and grieve.

But nevertheless, believe
Dostoyevsky got it right.
Come bask in the divine light.

Let's be Brazen and Alert

like the neighborhood deer
grazing well-tended gardens
for their midnight dessert.

Let us, if we will, be subtle
and soothing as chamomile,
as settled as a nettle by the river.

Let's be one minute flashy,
like a male cardinal against a blue sky,
the next invisible as a walking stick

clever as a magic trick.
Let's rasp on as persistently as cicadas
though summer's playing out—

no slippery syntax nor incongruous
dictions issuing from the mouth.
Let's be direct as the Vampire bat

homing in on its targeted host,
as curious yet cautious as the cat,
as devoted to one master (it's a biblical fact

we can never serve two) as the dog.
Let's linger all morning on a pond-side log
between a sunning turtle and a meditating frog.

From one moment to the next, let's not
forget it's miracles we should expect.
Like the ocean tossing out skeletons and broken shells,

let's empty out closets, dresser drawers and shelves
of all unneeded stuff—every last bit of frivolous fluff.
Alas, let's burn the brightest yet—

even as we begin to forget, the body
turns toward death, and we set our sights
on the other side of life.

To Die with Life

> *From the middle of life onward, only he remains vitally alive who is ready to die with life.*
> ~ Carl Jung

Torn this early morn between
two desires: to make the world
a better place; or to bask in nature's grace.
To turn away from all the destruction,
exploitation and abuse, or face it head on
and use the words of Isaiah to inspire—
the prayers of native Americans,
the warning of Hildegard of Bingen:
If we misuse (abuse) creation,
God's justice permits creation to
punish humanity. Sadly, those not
guilty are the ones most suffering.

Oh, to be a gannet—maritime,
spending most of my time
in the air, attached to nothing,
diving fabulously for fish.
I wish. But I'm torn, sworn
to do my part though my heart
is broken—all natural entities
    suffering.

Still, I'd sail away on silent skies,
down a silent hill, or skate
across a frozen lake, not daring
to break the silence. My preference.
But I must face the day's tumultuous
noise—the mind staggering while
the heart practices God's presence
as Brother Lawrence taught me to do.
Torn, but sworn by the grace of God

to enter into myself, and to accept
(forgive) all who kill to live,
or because they do not know
            what they do.

Feast of the Annunciation

Created free, we have not used
our freedom well. We have refused
to make a just and equal world—
pillaging the earth, robbing the poor,
colonizing and terrorizing the vulnerable.

Oh there have been (are) a few who've
tried (are trying) to stem the tide, but still
too many members of indigenous tribes
have died (are dying) trying to defend
their land. What we need these days

is more of us casting a personal gaze
on suffering people, willing to
accompany them, *this art . . . which*
teaches us to remove our sandals
before the sacred ground of the other.

What we need is more of us walking with
those for whom greed is the enemy they
fight against for the right to remain on their
land, more of us in the ministry of presence
where we can grasp the struggles,

encourage the possibilities, actively practice
patience, live dangerously (evoking Dorothy
Stang shot six times defending the Amazon).
Created free, how can it be we give up so easily
on reshaping the heartbreaking world?

Ponder the three wounds:
contrition, compassion, yearning
for God. The Equinox is over,
light once more has conquered darkness
and is shining in every creature.

We could be one in such a light as this.
Imagine it, make it so—simple and bright
as a red dragonfly poised on the shaft
of a hoe. Tell yourself no, it's not too late
to care, even though we're losing

seventeen species an hour, and the Amazon
is going, going, gone. Still, put on
your bravest face, and brace
for the fight of your life in this white
darkness, or dark whiteness,

depending on your perspective.
And reflect on this: the risk
of death is nothing compared
to the sickness of indifference and
forgetfulness of our collective past sins.

Ask to be forgiven, then vow to dig in,
no matter how impossible it seems to right
the wrongs. Sing a new song of hope,
recalling the Shawnee and Tecumseh.
Pray for a new day when we'll all be worthy

of being created free.

Elegy for the Tibetans Who Chose Self-immolation

Nothing so noble,
so admirable as *the power*
of the powerless,
nothing so liberating
as *living in truth.*
To set oneself ablaze

is to break the chains,
grasp the glory of
transcendent power.
Sixty years of cultural genocide—
repressive rule,
deliberate subversion—

who wouldn't decide
to douse himself with kerosene,
light a match, make a scene
in the marketplace,
at a road crossing,
on a bridge?

One hundred and sixty
since 2008 choosing to self-immolate—
an act for Tibet's freedom
and happiness. How to keep
on the middle path between
the world's reality and vacuity?

This is about light and dark,
order and chaos,
yin and yang,
doing the noble
liberating thing when
the moment arrives.

Acknowledgments

I am grateful to the editors of the following journals, in which some of these poems first appeared, at times in slightly different versions.

Adanna: "Territorial Disputes"
Aurorean: "Enduring Burning," "Released into the Light"
Beltway Poetry Quarterly: "After Reading *Steps Toward a Small Theory of the Visible* by John Berger"
Cold Mountain Review: "Imbolic (Candlemas) Day," "Subhanallah"
Connotation Press: An Online Artifact: "Everglades History Lesson One"
Copperfield Review: "Returning"
Cutthroat, A Journal of the Arts: "We are Not Gods"
Elusions: Refugee Poems (an anthology): "Elegy for the Tibetans Who Chose Self-Immolation"
Freshwater: "Clinging"
Jellyfish Whispers: "Secret to Positive Thinking"
La.Lit: "Red-legged Kittiwakes"
Passager Journal: "On the Feast Day of St. Clare"
Peacock Journal: "Hope'
Pensive: A Global Journal of Spirituality & the Arts: "Come Bask in the Divine Light," "To Save Us From the Dark"
Pigeon: "Anatomy of Empathy," "Camels Going to Market"
Plainsongs: "Let's Be Brazen and Alert"
Poets Without Borders: "Feast of the Annunciation"
Puget Sound Papers: "At the Edge of the Arabian Sea"
Pyrokinection: "Envisioning Mercy"
Raven Chronicles: "Called Out by Bulbuls"
Relief: A Journal of Art and Faith: "To Die with Life"
Spiritus: A Journal of Christian Spirituality: "Keeping Silent"
Talking River Review: "If Only"
The Poetry Society of Virginia Centennial Anthology: "No Death," "To Life"
The Sixty Four: Best Poets 2018: "Fire Raging, Questions Blazing"
Thin Air: "Little Tern"
Tiger's Eye Journal, (Infinities series #17, *Near the Arctic Circle*): "For the Birds Near the Arctic Circle"

The following poems appeared in *Beggar in the Everglades* (chapbook), Finishing Line Press: "Everglades History Lesson One," "Returning"

The following poems received awards:

"Aggression, A History Lesson" (previously entitled "Collared Versus Laughing Doves") —1st Prize, Judah, Sarah, Grace and Tom Memorial, Poetry Society of Virginia Contest, 2014

"Elegy for the Tibetans Who Chose Self-Immolation" —Finalist, 2019 Carolyn Forche Prize, WaterWood Press

"Feast of the Annunciation" —2nd-place winner of the 2020 Anita McAndrews Award.

"Fire Raging, Questions Blazing" —1st-place winner of the 2017 Daniel Varoujan Award (New England Poetry Club), judge: Fanny Howe

"For the Birds near the Arctic Circle" —1st place, Category 12, 2017 Poetry Society of Virginia annual contest, judge: Lisa Russ Spaar

"On the Feast Day of St. Clare" —Honorable Mention, *Passager's* 2020 Poetry Contest

"Watching Zebras and Doves" —2nd Prize winner, 27th Annual Artists Embassy International's Dancing Poetry Festival Contest

"We are Not Gods" —Finalist, 2021 Joy Harjo Poetry Award, *Cutthroat, A Journal of the Arts*

Notes

page 11, "The Ecopoet's Prayer" —In stanzas six and seven, the request ("ask of my reader that she invite the animals, birds and fishes to teach her") is in reference to Job 12:7–8 of the *Holy Bible.*

page 15, "Called Out by Bulbuls" —*Doing nothing, yet nothing left undone* is from the *Tao Te Ching.*

page 17, "Little Tern" —*"step aside from all thinking"* is from the late sixth-century Chinese poet Seng-Ts'An. He was the third patriarch of Zen in China.

page 19, "Aggression, a History Lesson" —Laughing doves (in the fifth stanza) is another name for Palm doves.

page 25, "For the Birds Near the Arctic Circle" —*Aye, on the shores of darkness there is light,*
And precipices show untrodden green . . . is from *To Homer* by John Keats.

page 27, "We are Not Gods" —*The whole land . . . a desolation* is from Jeremiah 4:27 of the *Holy Bible.*

page 29, "Vulturine Guineafowl" —In stanza five, the line "And I, driven out of Eden and alone," is a reference to Genesis 3:18 of the *Holy Bible.*

page 41, "Anatomy of Empathy" —In stanza two, "They say this Asian elephant" is a reference to researchers whose findings were published in *Current Biology Journal.* Lindner's sanctuary for homeless parrots (in stanza five) is located in Serenity Park, Los Angeles, CA.

page 43, "Ray of Darkness" —The Formosan clouded leopard was declared extinct 2013, the last confirmed sighting 1983. Sudan died March 19, 2018, in Kenya. In the last stanza, "ray of darkness" is taken from John of the Cross.

page 45, "Camels Going to Market" —The italicized phrase in the last line, *appareled in celestial light*, is taken from "Ode on Intimations of Immortality from Recollections of Early Childhood" by William Wordsworth.

page 47, "Territorial Disputes" —In stanza five, the italicized words are taken from John Lennon's song *Imagine*.

page 50, "Empty" —the statistics in stanza three are taken from the website of World Animal Foundation: https://www.worldanimalfoundation.com/advocate/wild-earth/params/post/1286260/an-elephant-killed-every-15-minutes

page 53, "Since Svalbard's Discovery," —The italicized words in the final stanza are taken from T. S. Eliot's poem "Ash Wednesday."

page 59, "Twelve Days in the Tongass," —In stanza four, the idea that "everything merits deliverance" is a reference to Romans 8:18–23 of the *Holy Bible*.

page 61, "Everglades History Lesson One" —The last stanza is a reference to Jeremiah 4:23–28 of the *Holy Bible*.

page 67, "Imbolic (Candlemas) Day" —A five-bu candlestick refers to a Japanese renga written in the time it takes for a candle to burn down five bu (half an inch)

page 67, "Imbolic (Candlemas) Day" —See *TIME* magazine article, March 22, 2011, for the story of "those brave young Syrians stirring an uprising."

page 71, "Beyond All Hunger and Ambition"—In stanza four, the italicized lines are from Rainer Maria Rilke's *Book of Hours: Love Poems to God*.

page 72, "Beyond All Hunger and Ambition" —the Tibetan word *lunga* refers to the Tibetan concept of windhorse.

page 75, "In between *Haram* and *Halal*" —In Arabic, *haram* means "impermissible to use or engage in according to Islamic law," and *halal* means "permissible." In stanza five, "to do an atom's weight of good" is a reference to the last verse, chap. 99 of the *Holy Qur'an*.

page 79, "Nature's Revered Teachers" —The last line, "all creation groaning for salvation," is a reference to Romans 8:19–23. See http://www.baylor.edu/content/services /documentphp/106707.pdf page 3: "Paul vividly depicts the present suffering of nature due to the Fall. 'The creation was subjected to futility, not of its own will but by the will of the one who subjected it' (v. 20). As a result, creation is in 'bondage to decay' (v. 20) and 'has been groaning in labor pains until now' (v. 22). Although the natural world is not itself fallen or disobedient to God, Adam's sin brought the created order into bondage to death, decay, corruption, and futility (vv. 20–21). As a result, creation is in "bondage to decay" (v. 20) and "has been groaning in labor pains until now" (v. 22).

page 81, "These Days" —The last line in stanza five is a reference to Meister Eckhardt.

page 83, "The Secret to Positive Thinking" —The italicized words in stanzas three and four are a reference to Felix Guattari's *The Three Ecologies*, found in the Introduction by Ian Pindar and Paul Sutton.

page 85, "In Search of my Own Hazelnut" —The Julian referred to in line one of the poem is Julian of Norwich.

page 87, "To Life" —The words *ruthless compassion* in stanza four are taken from Trungpa Rinpoche.

page 95, "Feast of St. Brigit" —The italicized lines in the first and second stanzas, *hurt not the earth, neither the sea nor the trees*, are from Revelation 7:3 of the *Holy Bible.*

page 99, "I Turn My Face to the Sun" —In the first stanza, HFA is Humane Farming Association.
In 1986, 3.5 million veal calves were slaughtered; in 2014, fewer than 600,000 were slaughtered.

page 107, "Hope" —Stanza one refers to Emily Dickinson's famous line/poem, "Hope is the thing with feathers."

page 115, "To Die With Life" —The italicized lines in the first stanza, *God's justice permits creation to punish humanity*, are from the *Holy Bible,* Isaiah 24:4–5.

page 117, "Feast of the Annunciation" —The italicized words in the third stanza, *this art . . . which teaches us to remove our sandals before the sacred ground of the other*, are from Pope Francis, 2013, describing accompaniment.

page 117, "Feast of the Annunciation" —The three wounds listed in the sixth stanza (contrition, compassion, yearning for God) are those Julian of Norwich described.

page 119, "Elegy for the Tibetans Who chose Self-Immolation" —The italicized words in the last stanza are those of Vaclav Havel.

IRON
PEN

"O that my words were written down!
O that they were inscribed in a book!
O that with an iron pen and with lead
they were engraved on a rock forever!"
—*Job 19:23–24*

Outcast and utterly alone, Job pours out his anguish to his Maker. From the depths of his pain, he reveals a trust in God's goodness that is stronger than his despair, giving humanity some of the most beautiful and poetic verses of all time. Paraclete's Iron Pen imprint is inspired by this spirit of unvarnished honesty and tenacious hope.

OTHER IRON PEN BOOKS

Andalusian Hours, Angela Alaimo O'Donnell
Begin with a Question, Marjorie Maddo
The Consequence of Moonlight, Sofia Starnes
Cornered by the Dark, Harold J. Recinos
Eye of the Beholder, Luci Shaw
Exploring This Terrain, Margaret B. Ingraham
From Shade to Shine, Jill Pelaez Baumgaertner
Glory in the Margins, Nikki Grimes
Idiot Psalms, Scott Cairns
Iona, Kenneth Steven
Litany of Flights, Laura Reece Hogan
Raising the Sparks, Jennifer Wallace
There Is a Future, Amy Bornman
To Shatter Glass, Sister Sharon Hunter, CJ
Wing Over Wing, Julie Cadwallader Staub

ABOUT PARACLETE PRESS

Paraclete Press is the publishing arm of the Cape Cod Benedictine community, the Community of Jesus. Presenting a full expression of Christian belief and practice, we reflect the ecumenical charism of the Community and its dedication to sacred music, the fine arts, and the written word.

SCAN TO READ MORE

www.paracletepress.com

You may also be interested in...

www.paracletepress.com